A History of Disappearance

Sarah Lubala

First published by Botsotso in 2022

59 Natal St
Bellevue East
Johannesburg 2198

Email: botsotso@artslink.co.za
Website: www.botsotso.org.za

ISBN: 978-1-990922-60-2

Design and text: Vivienne Preston

Previous publication(s) of poems:

As You Like It: Vol. II: The Gerald Kraak Anthology; Apogee Journal and The Heart of the Matter: Vol. III: The Gerald Kraak Anthology; Missing Slate's special issue: Poems Against Borders; A Women's Thing; Botsotso 18: Poetry from Public and Private Places; The Scores; Birds Thumb; Brittle Paper; The Shallow Ends; Entropy: The Talking Cure.

Photographs: page

For my brother J.

Contents

6 Errant Thoughts on Being a Refugee

1

on the worst of my days
this body is a gimcrack-vessel
no more than two lungs and
a tremor
nailed to salvaged wood

2

grief travelled with me
across the Ubangi River

i prayed love
and all her cognates
on the passage over:
libet (to please)
lips (to be needed)
lyp (to beg)

i arrived with
bruised knees
wet hair
a mouth-full of salted fish

3

i am so
hungry
hungry
hungry
for holiness
for communion
for a God you can sink
your teeth into

4

i was raised
on the Congolese-gospel
i can teach you how to forget
where you are from

to worship the wide road before you
hands open
like this:
make each palm
a letter
to the sky

5

Beni is a town
with one police station
airport
market
many graves

i should go back
my people are weeping

6

'home'
is a narrow bed

Boy with the Flying Cheekbones

Dear Théophile,
I imagine your bed
still smells like burnt sugar
and keen aching.
I cannot cross the threshold,
that room is steeped in a fever so ravenous –
it devours the air.

Lately,
I've been thinking about all the hungers
in men's chests
because of something about absence
and the heart growing fonder.

Dear Théophile,
You and I belong
to the same bruised piece of earth.
The rivers,
and anthems,
and old names
are in you.

Still, I smell
the hot bread,
the overripe mangoes,
the filthy currency.

Still, I feel
the sweltering April sky,
the villages aflame,
the potholes like wounds
in my side.

Dear Théophile,
Where are you now?
Where will this find you?
How do I tell you your hands were scripture
in full bloom,
each finger a slender verse.
I knew nothing of such kindness,
mercy me.

Though I have not seen them in years
I pray they can still make:
okra soup
ginger beer
wenge-figurines
a fist
a plea.

Théophile,
of all the prayers
commit but one to memory:
me before you.

Théophile,
you bury me.

Portrait of a Girl at the Border Wall

All the women in my life are hungry

I have written this one hundred times.
I do not know how else to tell it:
the girl by the roadside,
the bruised peach,
the narrow collar,
the night full of birds.

Her body is a long river
that cuts through every room.

See her in the kitchen,
see her standing behind the gate,
see how she cups her hands
for soap,
for bread,
for sweet milk.

Tell me,
where do I put her?
This girl pressed against the border,
this girl swallowing her papers whole,
this girl bird-wailing through a fence.

See her hands
holding the broken saucer,
stitching the skirt's hem,
cradling the last orange,
begging the names of God.

Where do I put her?

Tell me what is owed.
Here, the fist of hair.
Here, the cut lip.
Here, the legs;
split like fruit.

Who will take her?

This sorrow-of-home-girl,
this river-of-bees-girl,
this night-singing-girl,
this throat full of ghosts.

What to Say to the Immigration Officer When He Asks You Where You Are From

Say you left in a hurry,
say the days stumbled blind,
say the high grasses,
say the raw-boned women feeding babies
in the field.

Say the belly of the dry season,
say the lash of the earth,
say you swallowed whole countries,
say you spit only ash.

Say you were twenty-two in all,
say half were lost in the first week,
say you prayed to die young,
say you lived on and on.

On the Xenophobic Attacks in Johannesburg

They say God's promises
are yes
and Amen.

Who prayed for rope
and fire?

Confession

I

My father tried to kill his first wife
in a house with wide windows
and yellow hibiscus.

II

My love does not know
I have never stood naked
before a man.

III

For weeks I have tried to write an essay
on 'Black Death and Elegy';
I composed letters instead:

Maman,
I am writing to you from across the water
the years have been a heavy tide
against the shore of me.

IV

So much sits on the throat;
the men on roadsides,
the men in corridors.
My wrists are living birds,
small and keening inside me.

V

My uncle,
gone some twenty years,
telephones at dinner to tell me
he was once a child soldier.

Oh Lord,
the years kneel down.

A Burial Hymn

I

I am gathering from scratch.
Telling the stone house,
the thatch roof,
the leaden gun,
the months of rice and milk.

II

Oh Lord,
that I belonged to any land but this,
that I could not read the currents,
that the dirt knew nothing of me.

In these lines
I have tried to forget the words by which we are known.

III

I am told my poems hold too much water,
are too insistent in their weeping,
but I know nothing else.
Honeyed water for the mouth,
lemon water for the throat,
saltwater for the wounds.

History is the dog at my back,
hard by the heels;
the stain of red earth along the hem of every skirt.

IV

The night my grandfather died
I stood in a long line at Home Affairs
awaiting a new name.

Forgive me.

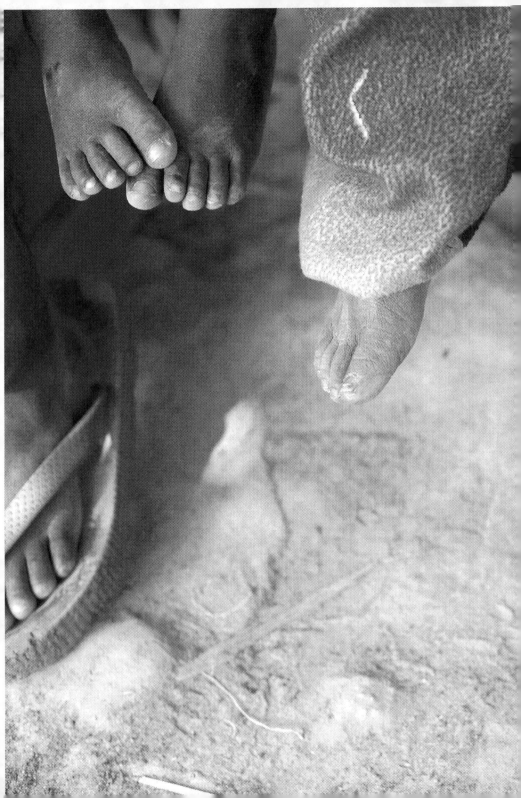

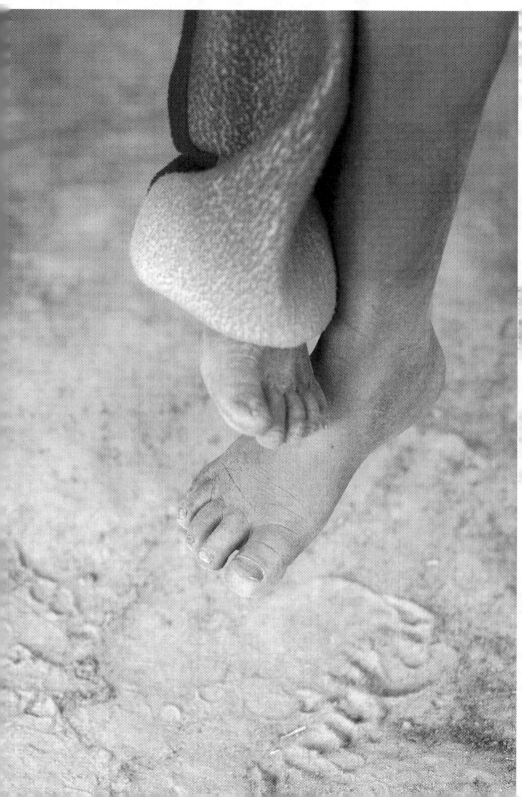

An Inheritance

I don't remember how it began.
With water or without?
With trembling or without?
Satisfied or fainting?

How might we measure it?
The dregs of a season;
one white confetti bush,
the salt on your hands,
an armchair
honeyed in winter light.

Did we sigh for the ease of it?
Did we think ourselves free?
As though our mothers are not ghosts,
as though this language is not a haunting.

There is a power in calling a thing by its proper name.
Not 'infidelity . . . '
Let us say
a history of disappearance,
let us say
men forget their names.

Not 'a black man hits his black wife.'
Let us say
she is alone in a room;
let us say
she is a rose in bloom.

What of your names?
He who came by water and blood,
bright edge of the knife,
worn-knot of breath,
bees in the throat.

A History of Disappearance

There are days
we can't go back to –
the summer the river ran dry,
a row of white jacaranda,
the mouth of March
bruised with longing.

How foolish we were
to refuse our inheritance;
the long rope of men in our blood,
our fathers' weaknesses.

How the days steal all they can;
the gap in my teeth,
my mother's humour,
whole volumes of poetry.

You
who asks too much,
who eats the air —
call off your dogs,
let me sleep

The Women
— *for Karabo Mokoena*

There is never enough water,
only the memory of it,
only the burning wood,
only the soft scuttle of mice trapped in the roof.

We are tired of the men –
in cars,
in markets,
in line at the post office.

The days are bone-dry,
we burn in our sleep;
our very being is a running knot,
tightening.

What is this sickness
that eats the bones of daughters?
Is there no balm?
Is there no physician here?
What can be done for the wound?

Spare us your burial hymns,
your murmured intercessions,
your tears.

Give us back our mouths.

The Rape of Hagar

So Hagar named the Lord who spoke to her, "You are the God who sees me,"
for she said, "Here I have seen the one who sees me!" — Gen 16:13

Tell me you wept,
tell me you were overcome with weeping,
that you return ever to it;
this moment that bleeds into all others,
river swallowing rivers,
I am soaked through.

Tell me you knew what it was according to the cry of it,
tell me it stripped the rooms bare;
this voice of rats and mice,
walls white to the bone,
the brown ankle,
slim blade of the caping knife,
the slow strangle of blackbirds,
rise of the mobbing call.

Tell me you sought it,
the span of a man's appetite,
this gnawing that makes a woman,
this giving,
the taking away.

Love, Again

"I tell you this to
break your heart,
by which I mean only
that it break open and never close again
to the rest of the world."
                    — *Mary Oliver*

In this way
the heart is broken, again.

Mosquito at the window
troubling the heat,
tender bite
pressed sore at the wrist.

Slowly, again.
        Slow pain,
        slow bleed of honey
        filling this small cup.

There are long walks, again;
the sky in half-light,
the barn swallows riding at dusk.

Again, the earth hangs on nothing;
again, we are caught;
again, the quiet breathing of all things.

Where does such knowledge come from?
Thin love,
scrawny thing,
how do you do it?
The hand reaches out again,
you don't bare your teeth.

A Leaving Song
— in memory of my great grandmother

The cows are dying in the fields, kokolo;
there is no meat this summer,
she is sold to an old chief, kokolo;
her legs sing blood and water.

She buries two babies, kokolo;
two bundles in white muslin,
the shroud is caught in the thorn bush, kokolo;
none but God can mend the tear.

She remembers her own mother, kokolo;
she recalls her bird-bone hands,
they dug in wild hunger, kokolo;
the earth never did yield.

There are rows of wild mangos, kokolo;
she moves hands and knees between them,
the night becomes the singing, kokolo;
nothing scares her anymore.

Honeymoon

In L'Isle-sur-la-Sorgue,
spring slips its bindings
and the island seems a girl
who has never known grief.
At the patisserie,
the old woman gifts us a baguette,
we share our luck with the birds.

For days we've moved like a long-held secret,
when at last, we are alone
it comes as a flight of swallows,
our bodies hunting on the wing.

This morning I know what it means to find favour
in God's sight;
the years have broken my bones,
now my name rises from the grave.

There is the fact of my illness,
days of a pain so large the earth sounds with it.
I finger each pill,
'It must be hard living in your head.'
Yes, my love. Which is to say, I'm lonely.
It is impossible to share a person's hunger,
impossible to share another's pain,

Tender and Only Beloved,
show me how our bodies are hidden in each other;
say touch is the only way of knowing;
say we are kept for better days.

Heliotrope

It's been fifteen years
and I'm still hunting all the places
where I put the memory of your name.
We'd sleep on the veranda in high summer,
hear monkeys screeching in the dark,
your hand on my leg loosened a clot of cicadas in my blood.

I can't pry your fingers from anything I say or do,
you are the ghost of my life,
the face in every white sheet,
devil in the needlework,
the hand braced against the flame.

Dear heart, be quick and come,
close as a curse,
urgent as the twist of cotton between my legs;
to the hungry soul,
every bitter thing is sweet.

Come home whole,
shame the bed.

New Braamfontein

In the vanishing dark
the call of the muezzin grieves the sky,
from the balcony, our neighbour cries into her phone:
"This city will break your heart."

Untouched by the emergency,
we grow lush among the house plants.
The flowering loaves number our days;
the laughing doves bring us the world.

In bed, a sovereign nation of two,
I turn to you:
"If you hate Johannesburg,
you've never been in love."

Ode to Spring

Here is
the breath of paper wrapping,
the soft rustle of prayer
for the swelling in the knees,
for two small bruises on the breast,
for the air at first light –
hungry and roaming.

Here is
the first clean bite of mint,
quince pear on the windowsill,
the slow aria of vanilla,
the notes so open
you could weave the sweetness in.

Here is
the porcelain bowl,
the daydream of water,
skin the colour of baked nectarines
in the bleached sea light.

Here is
the wet grass,
the heaven and the earth,
the bright throat of spring
yawning across the sky.

There are Days We Live as if Death Were Nowhere in the Background

During the Pittsburgh synagogue mass shooting
the rabbi spoke between *aliyahs*.

"Move away from the windows."
"If we have to evacuate, use all the doors."

After the final reading
he made one last announcement:
"We're trying to get a police presence here."

The service never stopped.

What do you call this?
When hearts go willingly down to the bars
of Sheol.

The bird hours
when words are for the wind;
before you speak
you are answered,
before you ask
you are heard.

A List of Things I Don't Tell My Mother

a)   i like to think of the black men in those shaving commercials. foam glistening down their chins. throats you could practice hunger on.

b)   i don't pray the way the nuns taught us. i left my rosary in uncle paulin's car on that trip to kananga 3 years ago. i've only just remembered.

c)   there is skin more tender than daylight just behind the ear. i plant two kisses on the indian girl i met on tinder. her laughter is clean water.

d)   love is not always the thick mouth of thunder. sometimes it is living bread. a slow white dream rising in the light.

e)   my affliction is not quite insomnia. i am only afraid to fall asleep. always the same dream. always the dimly lit corridor. always the smell of fresh snow. always the hand in my shirt. always begging. begging.

f)   most days i hate to be touched. every hand is my father's. you at the bottom of every staircase. a halo of blood around your neck.

g)   i want to write it. i never want to think of it again. the rabid years of girlhood. the chipping yellow paint. the house that held its breath.

h)   i think now i am a woman because i am terrified of my own body. what it makes men do.

My Tears Have Been My Bread

I'm sorry,
I broke it:
the treasured plate,
the delicate tile,
a full bowl
wrung out.

My hands are trembling again.
Too much sugar or
the salt of the last bite,
red meat,
not enough sun or exercise.

Too much water;
my tears have been my bread.
The waves rise so that the small boat
is covered.
God himself is asleep.

And these hands.
What are they for?
You can't trust them.
Pills bleed from them.
They smell of ditches
and men in cars.
The last time you felt loved.

This teacup
is the whole world.

Dispatch from Ward C

i

On Tuesday
you wake;
walk the backstairs to find a bird
half dead and thrashing,
stunned by its own purpose.

You count the split wing,
the muffled heart –
smallest of all seeds.

ii

The corridors are the loudest,
an artery of wailing.
What nicks the heart,
drawn tight across all things?

iii

I've known rage
the height of a woman,
the cloying scent of relaxer
holds the strongest memory;
the sweet scabbing,
the hairdresser's instructions:
'Let me know when it starts to burn.'

iv

I think often of your world,
the quotidian washing,
the nightly mewling of the street cat,
the sun-blind luck of ordinary days.

v

My old roommate had a razor blade
secreted in her bra.
What had the years been to her?
She read her Bible nightly,
repeated the words:
'Burn for burn, wound for wound,
bruise for bruise.'

vi

There are rules,
'no hook-ups'.
I dream of scarred fingers
and stonewashed linen,
summering at the window;
how mere touch
is abundance in the lack.

vii

The doctor asks if I know anything of
'intergenerational trauma.'
I think of my great-grandmother,
thirteen and wed,
the chicken coup in
red earth,
the kneaded dough of girl-limbs,
the clutch of a doll in one arm,
a baby in the other.

viii

They all want to know
what I'll do when I'm 'out there'.
God with me: I'll die, and I'll return,
I'll wound, and I'll be wounded,
I'll swallow the white throat of fear.

Fever

In a Bali hotel room
I shed electricity,
some quirk of the medication tends and stokes,
kindles against me.

The tongue is also a fire;
through the year's slow teeth
all the days of my life speak against me.
See fire eat fire.
See it set the whole course of a life on fire,
and itself set on fire by hell.

I'll say *Walungu, Okapi,*
Le Grand Bouelvard . . .
Trace the old neighbourhood:
reach for the women on street corners,
the boats at *Maluku,*
slip the high grasses –
bright hare in the brush smoke.

On the bathroom's tiled floor,
I reach a dear friend:
"I'm dreaming of rivers," I say.
"And the high whistle of blue quails."

I keep seeing my mother;
she is younger now,
her body snagged on my brother's.
He is only four years old and racked with fever.
She is begging the memory of her own mother.

How do fires die?
We reach the end,
and cry out for the beginning.

Stitch

'Vaginismus', now termed 'Genito-Pelvic Pain or Penetration Disorder', is the involuntary contraction of the pelvic floor muscles. The tight muscle contractions makes coitus, and gynaecological examinations, difficult or impossible. The cause is often linked to sexual trauma and its definition has been expanded in light of new research and now incorporates pain, muscle tension and fear of penetration.

American Psychiatric Association. (2013). Diagnostic and statistical manual of mental disorders (5th ed.). Arlington, VA

i

"This is how you burn your underwear
so no witch can find it."
She leans forward,
bends into the bathtub,
the thread is snagged,
runs red along the seam.

ii

Remember the sight of the mountains
in that tiny apartment in Montreal?
You're in her bathroom trying to use a tampon,
slipping a spoon between the seed and fruit,
your breathing a needle
through the wrong side of the fabric.

iii

This is how he walks into the poem,
in a place too narrow for speaking,
where prayer is backed to the hilt.

iv

For a long time after
you run at mirrors until you disappear,
your pelvis thinning out,
a knife tracing the scar,
the fold so quick through the linen.

You Are Here

a. in the days after you left, the emptiness became our government. we owned a single mattress. we belonged to the floor. to the blunt charity of sleep.

b. in the Guardian, there is an article on tshiluba.
the journalist writes: "the failure of the language to be taught at school has resulted in the replacement of native words by French words". i want to say something about losing your way. about speaking to your mother and stumbling over your own name.

c. it's not the will to die. only to kill the thing. that girl in her school dress. eye of water. fist of violets. the wick split with blue light. i must wait her out. i go to lay down and there is a knife in the bed.

d. i like the word ghosting as active verb. how it turns loss to remembrance and remembrance to inheritance. how the smoke of a life goes up forever and ever.

e. in cape town, a friend points to a car guard, tells me 'they're all congolese'. i am a country wrung out. i am every person consumed out of their place.

Confession is Not Betrayal

Still there in the dresser drawer,
my mother's ring,
its ceaseless weeping,
the rugs and their tired stains –
all of childhood is blood-orange.

Nearer to the dust of the fire,
the rams' skins,
a veil of good linen,
the paper language of bougainvillea.

I've learned to skirt the shards of those early years;
the day my father turned to stone
and my mother turned to Jesus,
the hours spent asleep on my knees.

Confession is not betrayal,
this is how I save my life:
I loosen death's fist,
one finger at a time.

The Dregs of Love

The morning mist comes
and she tends her grief,
the noose of puckered skin,
the empty beds,
the rooms
swollen beyond words.

Dear-one,
What can be done with this handful of leavings?
I am only a girl, you see;
ashy-kneed, singing mass hymns,
mango juice on every dress.
I came up thin,
strained across three countries;
the world's deepest river is in my blood.

I have nothing to give you
but the blood in my fingers,
the life of my hands
that come in from the wilderness,
they come from a far-off place.

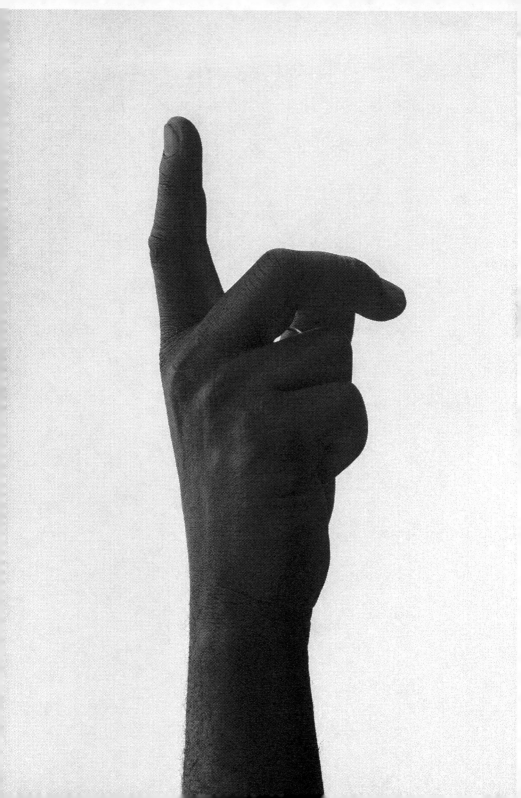

A List of Hauntings

1.

Home,
the slow current of hours,
a jug held white birds of paradise
still as my father's rage.

2.

His gestures lie over me;
my hands are not my hands
held closed against you.

3.

I am whatever you think a black woman is:
loose girl hit hard and straight,
the rope's nuisance,
our bodies are proverbs of ash;
every man's fire.

4.

I know how to tend silence,
how to rise before dawn and make a bed blind;
how to burn my own shadow,
how to close the seams of a life
and keep the fear of death in.

5.

I learned to love the way I learned to kneel:
as prayer or punishment.
The body prostrates itself
and the heart surrenders.

Questions you are Likely to Hear in an Asylum Interview

Where have you come from?

Think of a country,
lush-glazed and untouched.
Now imagine yours is the shape of that country,
the length of your body
a hungry man's dream.

Who harmed you or put you in fear of harm?

Out there,
terrors walk in men's skins.
Jackals at the door,
long nights and dogged need,
the stench of back roads in every bed.

Why did they harm you?

No woman belongs to herself,
you are a borrowed thing -
gold for the dowry,
snatch of river-song,
the shawl worn thin,
fasting within their sights.

Do you fear returning to your home country?

Freedom is your heart in the emptiness of night.
I pray to wake as a bird;
a song of sinews and feathers,
bright-winged and boundless,
loosed by God.

Water Woman

On the bus to Trieste
I marvel at the memory of water;
through the window,
the ocean's dark hem.

I think of that Croatian writer, Matvejević
who said of the Adriatic:
"It is a sea of intimacy."
I weep at every shore.

I am a girl of the river,
thick with silt and the smell of clean rain,
mist off the Uele,
green heart at my centre.

I come as the margin,
the stone's cursed edge;
Luba woman beating the clothes dry.

All the world survives in these bare arms.
Brown days stitched together,
tired as cloth,
rough as dog-howling.

The scream of marsh hens,
the vast waters
and the keening that rides it;
an ache as wide as what it holds.

I Take Myself to the Glory of Trees

This morning is a sharp thing;
I struggle to breathe past it and
circle the edge of tightening lungs.

On days like this
I depend on the intimacy of trees;
the birches shed their clothes,
their naked trunks bear the earth.
Life is the borrowing of soil I am not strong enough to dig;
I am too internal.
When the air thins to a strangle
I take myself to the glory of trees.

I remember Nakala,
that village deep in the heart of the Congo Basin,
a world filled with every green thing with which God
and men are honoured.
I stood high above the hills
where the mist burns off at mid-afternoon,
and my heart went into those woods;
and neither will pass away.

I am Never More Black

I am never more Black
than first thing in the morning,
my hair a knot of animals brawling,
biting at the comb.

When the man at the petrol station
demands to know why I don't speak an African language
what he really means is: perform your Blackness.
He means, show me you are not a burial place for our traditions.

In the 4th grade
an Irish nun tells me my braids are a distraction;
I'm sent home
to practice disappearance.

Years ago, on a crowded street in Hong Kong,
a Nigerian man sent me a tender nod of recognition
as if to say:
'See how Blackness grants us the power of ubiquity?'
We are everywhere at once.

Self Portrait with Chronic Pain

I.

At the brink of myself
I bend and buck like some fresh horse,
the woman in the mirror screams an animal scream;
but all that sounds is the crack of dead wood,
a chorus of embers between her teeth.

II.

It is enough now,
only a handful of flour in the bowl,
a little oil in the jar.
This raw-boned June
ache has teeth
and the air itself is complicit,
each breath makes an end of me.

III.

Tonight,
I am both the wound and the knife.
A fever consumes, but I am the fire.
I have bled every day for a year
and I am no witch,
though I have survived the pyre.

Elegy for Girlhood

I grew up a small hunger,
a prayer uttered into the ground,
formed slight and in secret –
a small cup of tremblings.

What can prepare you for the day childhood
is sent to the threshing floor?
Black barbies, mermaids and blue tulle skirts –
artefacts from a time not merely lost,
but cut away.

Now I am thirty and alive to my needs,
brought up from the dark.
In the astonishment of these after-years,
what is possible to ask from this life?

The Baker's Wife

Moves like a promise kept,
like the rise of good flour
in the fullness of the warmest hour.

Her lover,
sculptor of time,
practitioner of presence,
builds her up from bones.

This is how you hold her:
tend her soft in the fire,
weave the bright road of hair,
fold the sun of her waist against you.

She says: breathe me in,
scent of butter and dry sugared earth,
this smell that inspires kindness in strangers;
I welcome all men.

Early Morning Rain

It comes as a trick of daylight,
creeps into the bedroom quiet,
behind curtains of white linen
our bodies elude the dark.

What if this were enough?
These dust motes yoked to a rising sun,
the quickening of spring,
the air thickened with birdsong.

These are the good green days of September,
there is no thought of fire.
Where there was rot there is perfume,
where there was rope, thread.

The Litany of Mary

They're painting the walls of the Collégiale Notre-Dame-des-Anges;
inside, 122 gold angels usher the Virgin Mary forward.
In the slow bleed of dusk
I stand below its battered awning,
ever closer,
ever closer.

Mother,
grant me a secret language that is all our own.
I'll say snowfall in Old Quebec, and you'll know that I mean:
the man who found me in the dark,
twilight turned to trembling,
the months that ground my bones.

Our Lady of the Waiting Rooms,
I have lived thirty years gallows-scared,
touched by God or love or madness, depending.
I am a Sunday orphan,
child of the Ghost Kingdom,
begging honey from the rock.

Undoer of Knots,
loosen the secret pills inside my teeth,
the good medicine of meaning,
give me the words that are God
when I cannot see God.

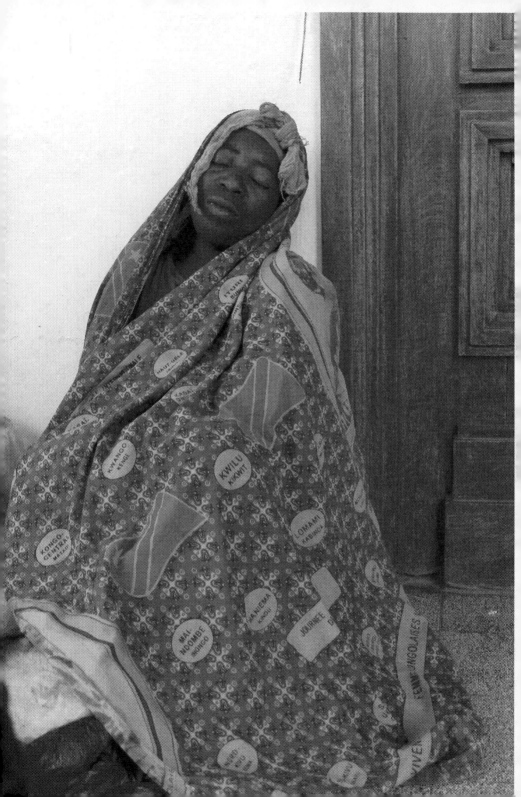

Desertion

How do you live if you can't love? And how can you live if you do?"
                                                    James Baldwin

Sometimes I dream you're already gone.
I wander through your leaving,
broken-necked in the arms of its shadow,
heart-sick and delirious,
widowed before your death

You say 'love' and a trap door opens,
inexorable and ravenous.
In the wet mouth of fear
I dare not say the word aloud,
I dare not think it.

I've grown tired of walking with a knife in my hand,
but this string of kin going or gone circles a long road.
They pass through me and hound me.
They bang on the windows when I am asleep.
They tap at the door.

I'd trade these desertions for anything —
tattered clothing, the last scrap of day, a stone, thin smoke.
I am a soft animal,
only a shudder of a girl
braced against all the ways I can be hurt.

To love is to confess the need of it,
and I do,
but I cannot be my mother,
faithful to her torturer,
begging for a crust of bread.

We don't belong to each other.
I belong to the alphabet of everything,
to the valley of vowels,
to myself.

Acknowledgements

This book would not have been possible without the patience and years-long support of its editor, Allan Kolski Horwitz. My mother, grandmother and great-grandmother served as inspirations for parts of this book. There aren't enough words for how much they mean and have meant to me. I'd also like to thank my family, especially my dad Louis and brother Elijah, for their encouragement. A huge thanks to my dearest friends who read many drafts and offered invaluable feedback. Lastly, thank you to my great love, Jaco, who continues to be my biggest cheerleader and confidant. Thank you for celebrating every iteration of this book with me.

Sarah Lubala is a Congolese-born poet. Her family fled the Democratic Republic of Congo two decades ago admidst political unrest as militant factions tried to overthrow the dictator Mobutu Sese Seko. Her family relocated first to Cape Town, South Africa, then Abidjan — the capital of the Ivory Coast — before returning to South Africa and settling in Johannesburg. She has since spent her life in various parts of Africa, Asia and Europe and believes herself to be from here, there, everywhere and nowhere. She currently lives in Johannesburg with her husband and cat.
Sarah has been twice shortlisted for the Gerald Kraak Award, and once for The Brittle Paper Poetry Award as well as longlisted for the Sol Plaatje EU Poetry Award. She is also the winner of the Castello Di Duino XIV prize.

Printed in the United States
by Baker & Taylor Publisher Services

date night

If I could have dinner with one person
Dead or alive
It would be my brain
Dead and alive.

I would tell it:
Breathe
It has passed.

Printed in the United States,
by Baker & Taylor Publisher Services